Do
Can't Read

by Robin Bloksberg
illustrated by Michael Sloan

Scott Foresman

Editorial Offices: Glenview, Illinois • New York, New York
Sales Offices: Reading, Massachusetts • Duluth, Georgia
Glenview, Illinois • Carrollton, Texas • Menlo Park, California

Ben has a little dog.

The dog can run and hop.

But the dog can't read.

They go for a walk.

Too bad the dog can't read!

The dog can't read a word.

5

Ben doesn't pick the flowers.

But his dog does!

The dog can't read.

Ben sits down to rest.

What does the dog see?